IMMIGRATION IN A CHANGING ECONOMY

ECONOMY

California's Experience—
Questions and Answers

KEVIN F. MCCARTHY

GEORGES VERNEZ

Prepared for the
Office of the Secretary of Defense, the California Business Roundtable,
The Ford Foundation, The William and Flora Hewlett Foundation,
the James Irvine Foundation, and The Andrew W. Mellon Foundation

National Defense Research Institute
Center for Research on Immigration Policy

RAND

This report summarizes in some detail the principal findings of a comprehensive study of how immigration has affected the state of California, the full details of which are documented in *Immigration in a Changing Economy: California's Experience*, by Kevin F. McCarthy and Georges Vernez (MR-854-OSD/CBR/FF/WFHF/IF/AMF, Santa Monica, CA: RAND, 1997). The research was funded by the Office of the Secretary of Defense, the California Business Roundtable, The Ford Foundation, The William and Flora Hewlett Foundation, the James Irvine Foundation, and The Andrew F. Mellon Foundation. Other, related reports include

- Robert F. Schoeni, Kevin F. McCarthy, and Georges Vernez, *The Mixed Economic Progress of Immigrants*, MR-763-IF/FF, Santa Monica, CA: RAND, 1996.

- Georges Vernez and Allan Abrahamse, *How Immigrants Fare in U.S. Education*, MR-718-AMF, Santa Monica, CA: RAND, 1996.

- Georges Vernez and Kevin F. McCarthy, *The Costs of Immigration to Taxpayers: Analytical and Policy Issues*, MR-705-FF/IF, Santa Monica, CA: RAND, 1996.

The research summarized here was carried out at RAND in the Center for Research on Immigration Policy in collaboration with the Forces and Resources Policy Center of RAND's National Defense Research Institute (NDRI). The Center for Research on Immigration Policy was founded in 1987 to provide a focal point for ongoing RAND immigration research being carried out by various disciplines and from different perspectives. NDRI is a federally funded research and development center sponsored by the Office of the Secretary of Defense, the Joint Staff, and the defense agencies.

Contents

Figures

The current national debate on immigration policy is especially intense in California, home to one-third of the country's immigrants. Much of this debate consists of advocates stating their views without the benefit of a nonpartisan assessment of the issue and the challenges it poses for the state. Our study provides such an assessment by examining how immigration has interacted with other demographic and economic trends in California since the 1960s. This three-year study, the first to take a 30-year perspective, profiles the changing character of recent immigrants and considers their contribution to the economy, their effects on other workers and the public sector, and their educational and economic success. Its findings can provide lessons for other states, the nation, and even other countries.

Key Findings

We found that despite changes in the characteristics of immigrants, California's employers continue to benefit from their presence. However, the size of current immigration flows—and the disproportionate share of poorly educated immigrants they contain—combined with changes in the state's economy has increased the costs of immigration to the state's public sector and to some native workers. Immigration's effects in the future will depend largely on whether the federal government alters its immigration policies to address the current changes and the state initiates proactive policies for integrating immigrants into its social and economic fabric.

The New Immigration

Immigration into California, both legal and illegal, has increased at unprecedented rates over the past 30 years. During the 1970s, more immigrants—1.8 million—entered the state than in all prior decades combined. That number doubled again to 3.5 million in the 1980s, and the 1990s rate has remained high despite a severe recession in the decade's early years. As a result, immigrants now constitute more than one-fourth of California's residents and workers and are responsible for more than half of the growth in the state's population and labor force.

The composition of the immigrant flow has also changed dramatically. About half of California's recent immigrants come from Mexico and Central America, and another third come from Asia. These groups are less educated, are younger, and have more children than immigrants elsewhere. They also are more likely to be refugees and undocumented. For all these reasons, immigration is affecting California more substantially than any other state in the nation.

Immigrants arrive with all levels of education, but on average their educational levels have declined relative to those of the native population. This decline is particularly significant, because the rate at which immigrants and their children succeed economically and socially depends directly on how educated they are. Highly educated immigrants reach economic parity with native residents within their lifetimes. Those with extremely low levels of education—mainly from Mexico and Central America and refugees from Indochina—command low earnings and make little economic progress in their lifetimes. Their limited prospects raise important concerns about whether and when their children will be able to reach parity with other groups.

The Economic Benefits

California's employers, and its economy in general, have been the main beneficiaries of immigration. Immigrants are paid less than native workers at all skill levels but are equally productive employees. As a result, they have contributed to California's faster economic growth compared to the rest of the nation from 1960 to 1990. Even when California's growth advantage disappeared during the depths of the 1990–94 recession—to which immigration did not contribute—immigrants continued to arrive in the state in great numbers and to hold down its labor costs.

The Costs

However, these economic benefits have not come without certain costs. A concentration of refugees and other low-income immigrants that make heavy use of public services has had a negative fiscal effect on California. The greatest and most enduring impact has been on the state's public education system: Predominantly of childbearing age and with fertility rates higher than those of the native population, immigrants have contributed significantly to the state's rapid increase in primary and middle school enrollments. The effect of this increase on the state's community colleges and universities has yet to be fully felt.

And there are other costs as well. Because the demand for low-skilled workers has been declining, the continuing influx of low-skilled immigrants has held down both the earnings and the job opportunities of the low-skilled labor force. Overall, California is losing low-skilled workers to other states, and between 1 and 1.5 percent of the state's adult native population has left the labor force or become unemployed because of competition from immigrants. Immigration has also contributed to the widening income disparity among the state's workers and to the loss of their educational advantage over workers nationwide.

Immigrants' Prospects

Recent changes in California's economy do not bode well for low-skilled immigrants. Employment growth recently picked up from what it was in the recession of the early 1990s, but it is not expected to return to the rapid pace it maintained prior to 1990. Moreover, as the state's economy has shifted to the higher-skill, service and technology industries, employers have begun to seek a more highly educated workforce. Between 1970 and 1990, 85 percent of California's new jobs went to workers with at least some postsecondary training. As the economic prospects of these well-educated workers improve, the prospects of the less educated diminish: They compete for fewer jobs and face slow growth in their career earnings. Finally, California-voter resistance to increasing taxes, exemplified by Proposition 13, has limited the funds available to the state and to local governments, leading to cutbacks of many programs.

When these factors are combined with continued high levels of immigration, the signposts all point to a widening gap between what the state's economy and public services can provide and what the growing numbers of poorly educated immigrants need. Given these trends, California will find it increasingly difficult to maintain—let alone improve—the prospects of low-skilled immigrants and their children and to ensure that immigration remains an overall benefit to the state's economy and residents.

Recommendations

The federal government sets the policies that determine how many and which immigrants enter California. We recommend that the federal immigration policies be changed to: (1) provide the flexibility needed to change immigrant quotas and entry criteria as needed to maintain modest levels of immigration and to emphasize the educational level of immigrants; (2) provide financial relief to states bearing a disproportionate share of costs associated with immigration; (3) control levels of illegal immigration; (4) recognize the special relationship between Mexico and the United States and expand U.S.-Mexico cooperation on immigration issues.

For California, we recommend that the state develop proactive policies for integrating immigrants both socially and economically. Since education is the most important determinant of the success of immigrants and their children, California must—above all else—make special efforts to promote high school graduation and college attendance for the children of immigrants, most of whom are born in the state. In addition, the state should work with the federal government to sponsor programs that encourage naturalization and expedite English proficiency for adult immigrants already living and working in California.

Chapter One

California Is a Test Case for National Immigration Policy

Context

California's transformation into a diverse racial and ethnic society through immigration has attracted the attention of the rest of the country and other parts of the world. Those who see California as a trendsetter for the rest of the nation are looking closely for clues about how such changes can best be managed. Others, perhaps less optimistic, are looking for clues about whether such a truly multiethnic society can indeed prosper and function peacefully.

The ambivalence many people feel about the changes taking place in California is palpable not only within the state, but in the country at large. The 1992 riots in Los Angeles were perceived by some as a natural outburst of the underlying tensions that the newcomers were creating. And when an unusually deep and long recession hit the state's economy early in the 1990s, some saw the backlash against immigration, symbolized by the passage of Proposition 187, as inevitable.

Since California's attraction to immigrants is nothing new, what explains the current focus on immigration? We think there are two changes that make the present situation different from what occurred before. First, the patterns of immigration into California have changed sharply over the past 30 years. For example, the number of immigrants has increased fivefold, and the mix of ethnic and socioeconomic groups has grown much greater. Second, California's economic environment has changed. The state's industrial base has shifted away from manufacturing toward service and high-technology industries whose employers place a greater premium on a more educated labor force. As a result, less-skilled workers have had to compete for a stable pool of lower-paid jobs and face the prospect of little growth in their career earnings. In addition, California's state and local governments have faced recurring fiscal crises, trying to meet residents' needs and demands with fewer and fewer resources.

Research Questions

Although the dynamics behind these two changes are largely unrelated, the combination of the two brings up important questions about recent immigration and its impact on California:

- To what extent can we generalize about immigration?

- How has immigration contributed to California's demographic profile?

- How successful are today's immigrants at integrating into California's economy and society?

- What role do immigrants play in California's labor force?

- Has immigration contributed to California's disproportionate economic growth?

- Has immigration affected workers in California?

- Do immigrants put a disproportionate demand on public services?

- Should federal and state policy toward immigrants and immigration be changed?

The rest of this report answers each of these questions in turn. Each chapter sets the context for the basic issue, poses the specific question, reviews our main findings, and briefly summarizes our conclusions.

Chapter Two

Care Must Be Taken in Generalizing About Immigration

Context

Federal immigration policy applies evenly to all immigrants (with important exceptions for refugees), and both politicians and advocates often talk about immigration as though it were an undifferentiated movement. The fact is, however, that immigrants come to the United States from all over the world. This is particularly true in California, home to one-third of the nation's immigrants and to more different kinds of immigrants than any other state.

Question

To what extent can we generalize about immigration?

Immigration has changed greatly over time.

First, recent immigration differs from earlier immigration in sheer numbers. Between 1960 and 1995, California's number of immigrants increased more than sixfold, from 1.3 to 8.0 million. Second, the origins of California's immigrant population have shifted (see Figure 2.1). Prior to 1960, most of California's immigrants came from Europe and Mexico; those from Asia and Central America were distinct minorities. Today, 70 percent of the state's immigrants come from Asia and Mexico, and there are about twice as many immigrants from Central America as from Europe.

California's immigrants differ from immigrants in the rest of the nation.

We found that

- The scale of immigration into California is unequaled anywhere else in the United States. One-third of the nation's immigrants live in California, and

3

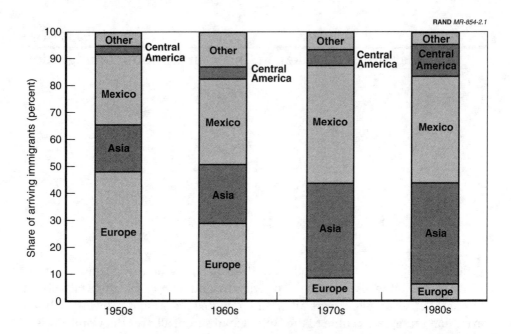

Figure 2.1—National Origins of California's Recent Immigrants Have Changed

they make up 22 percent of the state's residents. By contrast, immigrants constitute over 10 percent of the population in only four other states and less than 3 percent in most states.

- California's immigrants are younger. The average age of foreign-born California residents is 33, compared to 42 for immigrants elsewhere in the country.

- California's immigrants have arrived more recently. They have been in the United States only two-thirds as long as immigrants elsewhere in the nation: 11 versus 15 years.

- California's immigrants are less educated (see Figure 2.2). Over 40 percent of immigrants in California have less than a high school education, compared to 30 percent for all U.S. immigrants.

- California's immigrants differ in terms of national origins (see Figure 2.3). California receives 40 percent of its immigrants from Mexico, compared to 15 percent for the rest of the nation. California's immigrants are also twice as likely as immigrants elsewhere in the country to be Central American or Filipino. On the other hand, immigrants in the rest of the nation are much more likely to be from Europe and the Caribbean.

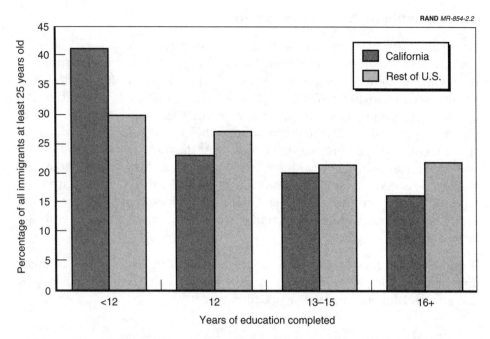

Figure 2.2—California's Immigrants Are Less Educated Than Other Immigrants

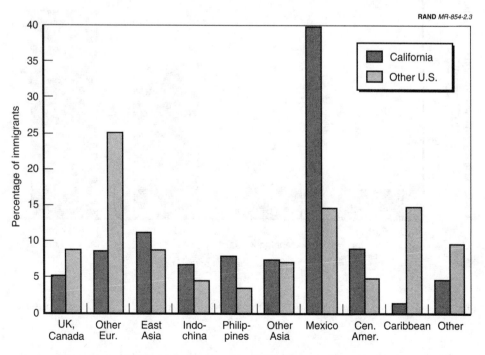

Figure 2.3—California's Immigrants Differ from Other Immigrants as
to National Origin

Immigrants from different places vary greatly.

The characteristics of immigrants from different places of origin vary sharply. California's immigrants can be sorted into four groups along a spectrum that distinguishes them by geographic region of origin and how their sociodemographic characteristics differ from those of U.S. natives. At one end of the spectrum is a group consisting of Europeans and Canadians. Members of this group are generally similar to natives in that they are older and well educated, speak English well, and have small families. At the other end is a group comprising Mexicans and Central Americans. Members of this group generally are younger, less well educated, and less likely to speak English well, and have large families. The two groups in between are the Indochinese, who fall closer to the Mexicans and Central Americans, and the other Asians, who fall closer to the Europeans and Canadians.

Figure 2.4 shows how the groups compare in terms of education—an important dimension relating to economic progress. Table 2.1 characterizes the groups along several dimensions relative to California natives.

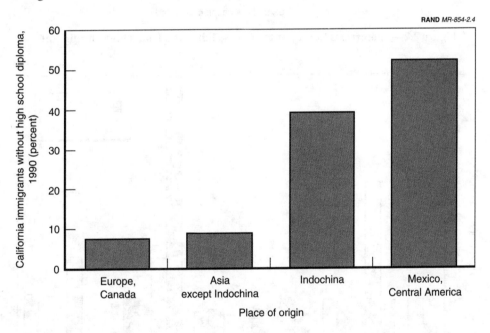

Figure 2.4—California Immigrants of Different Origins Vary in Educational Attainment

Table 2.1

California Immigrants of Different Origins Vary Along Many Dimensions

Place of Origin	Percentage of All Immigrants	Comparisons Relative to Natives				Entry Status
		Household Size	English Proficiency	Employment	Earnings	
Europe and Canada	14	Same	Close	Same	Same	Mostly legal
Asia except Indochina	25	Somewhat lower	Lower	Somewhat lower	Somewhat lower	Mostly legal
Indochina	6	Much larger	Much lower	Much lower	Much lower	Mostly refugee
Mexico and Central America	46	Much larger	Much lower	Same	Lower	Many illegal

Immigrants of different entry status also vary.

Although there are no census data on legal versus illegal immigrants,[1] we were able to reach some tentative conclusions based on the characteristics of those formerly illegal immigrants who were given amnesty as a result of the 1986 Immigration Reform and Control Act. We infer that, compared to legal immigrants, illegal immigrants tend to earn less, to be less proficient in English, and to be less educated generally. However, they are just as likely to be employed as are legal immigrants, and they are more likely to be employed than are refugees, who have the highest rate of dependence on public assistance.

The Short Story

Generalizations regarding immigrants should not be accepted uncritically. Differences among immigrants do exist, and policies dealing with immigrants must take them into account.

---

[1]Status can change over time. Legal entrants can become naturalized citizens, refugees can become permanent residents and eventually citizens, and illegal immigrants can become legal and also naturalize over time.

Chapter Three

Immigration Has Changed the Face of California's Population

Context

Before the 1970s surge in immigration, California's growth was driven largely by migrants from elsewhere in the United States, and its age structure resembled that of the rest of the country. Its ethnic diversity was already greater than that of the United States as a whole, but not by very much.

Question

How has immigration contributed to California's demographic profile?

Immigration is the largest component of population growth in California.

Immigration has replaced the interstate migration of U.S. natives as the principal component of growth in California's population. As Figure 3.1 shows, from 1940 to 1970, immigration accounted for less than 10 percent of the state's growth; but since 1970, that figure has risen to almost 50 percent. What Figure 3.1 does not show is the extent to which persons born in California (i.e., natives) are the children of immigrants. When they are included, immigration becomes responsible for about 67 percent of California's growth over the last 25 years.

The growth of the immigrant population has been felt unevenly across the state.

Immigrants have not settled evenly in California (see Figure 3.2). Southern California, particularly Los Angeles County (the state's most populous county), has become the place of residency for most of the state's recent immigrants. In 1960, immigrants made up about one in every ten residents in Los Angeles County; by 1990, that number had risen to one in every three.

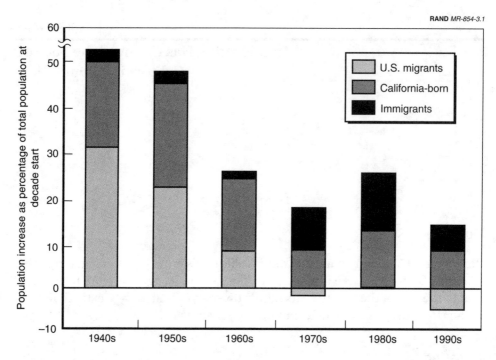

Figure 3.1—Immigrants Have Contributed Increasingly to California's Population
Growth

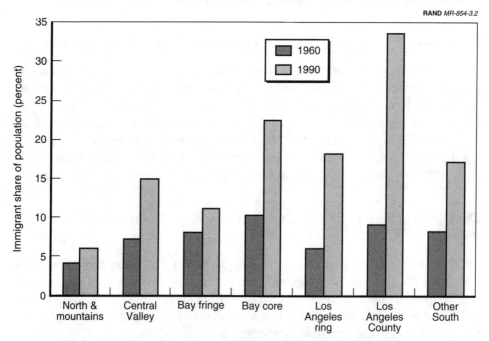

Figure 3.2—Recent Immigrants Have Settled Disproportionately in
Southern California

Immigration has kept California younger than the rest of the country.

The maturation of the baby boom generation has dominated America's age structure since the late 1940s. Baby boomers crowded the nation's schools during the 1960s and 1970s, flooded the entry-level labor market during the late 1970s and the 1980s, have been swelling the ranks of the nation's experienced workers during the 1990s, and will dominate the nation's retirees early in the second decade of the next century.

In 1990, the largest group of baby boomers was between the ages of 25 and 34, and its presence was clearly felt in both California and the nation (see Figure 3.3). However, the influx of immigrants, who tend to be primarily in their early adult years, has altered California's age profile. In 1960, the California and U.S. age profiles were virtually identical. As of 1990, they differed in that California had somewhat more children (age 15 or less), decidedly more young workers (age 25 to 34), and notably fewer retirees. Thus, immigration has made the state's population younger, and hence potentially more productive, than it would have been otherwise.

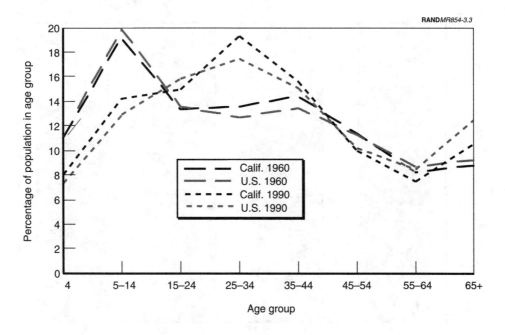

Figure 3.3—California Is Younger Than the Rest of the Country

California has become much more ethnically diverse than the United States as a whole.

In 1970, minorities made up roughly 20 percent of the population in both California and the United States as a whole (see Figure 3.4). In 1990, minorities were around 25 percent of the U.S. population but were approaching 50 percent of California's. Hispanics alone constituted about the same percentage of California's population that all minorities constituted for the entire nation: 25 percent. And about half of California's increase in Hispanics and most of its increase in Asians was the direct result of immigration.

The Short Story

Immigration has made Californians much different from what they were in the 1960s and much different from what they would have become had there been no immigrants. Indeed, even if immigration into California were to stop, its impact would continue to be felt for many generations.

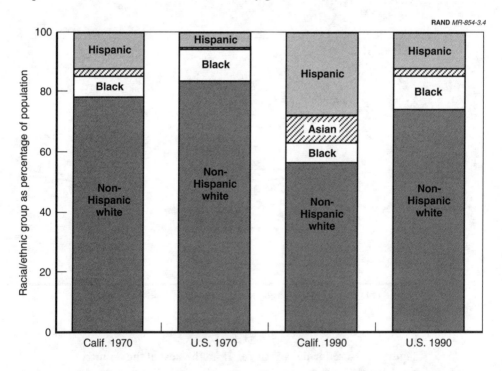

Figure 3.4—California Is Much More Ethnically Diverse Than the Rest of the Country

Chapter Four

The Success of Immigrants Increasingly Depends on Their Education

Context

Each wave of immigrants has usually taken at least two generations to reach full and equal participation in America's society and economy. In part, this two-generational aspect reflects the multidimensional nature of the process. When immigrants come to the United States, they are typically confronted with a host of challenges—learning a new language, getting a job and adjusting to a new labor market, and becoming familiar with a new society. The more time the immigrant spends in the new country, the more this adjustment takes place, but progress toward full and equal participation often continues into the next generations. The primary key to achieving participation is education, and the importance of that key is growing.

Question

How successful are today's immigrants at integrating into California's economy and society?

In earnings, immigrants have been losing ground to natives.

Taken as a whole, the earnings of California's immigrants are now lower than those of equally educated natives, and they have become progressively more so for immigrants having less than a college degree (see Figure 4.1). For example, in 1960, immigrants with only a high school diploma earned 6 percent less than equally educated natives; by 1990, that deficit had increased to 16 percent.

But such generalizations are misleading: Mexicans and Central Americans lag other immigrant groups in terms of earnings.

Broad trends such as those shown in Figure 4.1 convey useful information, but it must be remembered that they also conceal important distinctions. The

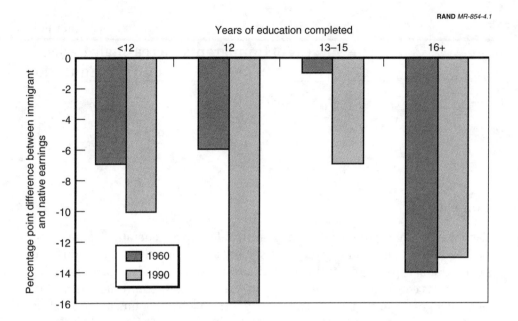

Figure 4.1—Earnings Gap Between California's Natives and Immigrants Is Growing

earnings of European and most Asian immigrants not educated in the United States increase fairly rapidly relative to those of natives. By the age of 30 to 35, these immigrants earn as much as or more than natives do (see Figure 4.2). In contrast, Mexican and Central American immigrants not educated in the United States experience flat or decreasing earnings after age 30, losing ground to natives as they age. Given that almost 50 percent of California's immigrants come from Mexico and Central America, this distinction is especially relevant.

Education is the key determinant of earnings.

Differences in earnings among immigrant groups are probably less a product of place of origin than of educational level. South American immigrants, for example, whose educational levels are much closer to those of Europeans than to those of other Hispanic groups, earn substantially more than other Hispanic immigrants do. At the other end of the spectrum, Indochinese immigrants, whose educational levels are much closer to those of Mexican and Central American immigrants than to those of other Asian immigrants, have low earnings.

Immigrants from different countries enter California with vastly different educational levels. As Figure 4.3 shows, most Mexicans immigrating into the

RAND*MR854-4.2*

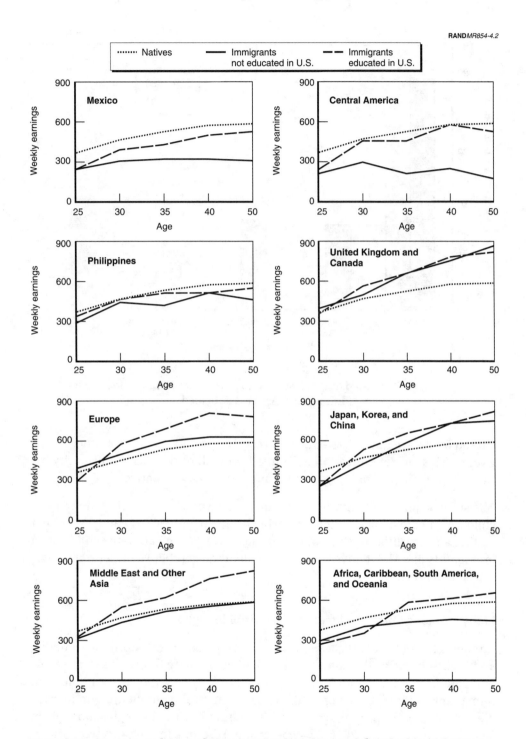

Figure 4.2—Mexican and Central American Immigrants Lag Other Groups in Earnings

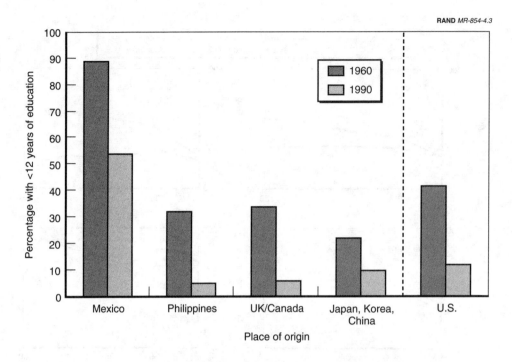

Figure 4.3—Compared to U.S. Natives and Most Other Immigrants, Mexican Immigrants Are Less Educated

United States are much less educated than U.S. natives and most other immigrants. This lack of education accounts for much of the income disparity between immigrants from Mexico and Central America and natives.

The story is quite different, however, for those who enter the United States as children and are educated here. Looking back at Figure 4.2, it can be seen that getting an education in this country closes most of the gap between Mexican immigrants and U.S. natives and almost all of the gap between Central Americans and natives.

Many Hispanic immigrant teens fail to enroll in high school.

Immigrants from most places of origin enroll in California's primary, middle, and high schools at the same rates as natives and are as likely as natives to graduate from high school. This is not true of Mexican and Central American immigrant children, however. Their enrollment rates begin to drop off in middle school and fall progressively further behind during the high school years (see Figure 4.4). By age 20, only 45 percent of Hispanic immigrants have gradu-

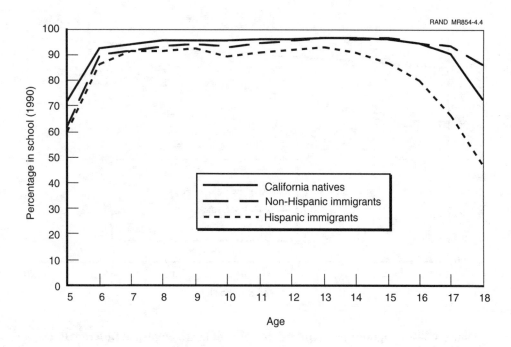

Figure 4.4—California's Hispanic Immigrant Teens Are Less Likely Than Other Teens to Be Enrolled in School in California

ated from high school, compared to 90 percent of non-Hispanic immigrants and 88 percent of natives. It appears that instead of dropping out of the school system in the traditional sense, many Hispanic immigrant adolescents never attend school at all—they have come north to find work, not to attend school.

Immigrants acquire English language skills at different rates.

Immigrants arriving in the United States differ substantially in their English skills, the differences being attributable to level of education and the frequency with which English is used in their homeland. All immigrants see an improvement in English skills as they remain in the country (see Figure 4.5), but the better-educated immigrants pick up English more quickly than their less-educated counterparts.

Subsequent generations show gains in education.

Given that some immigrant groups are not catching up to natives in earnings during the first generation, what are the prospects for the second and subse-

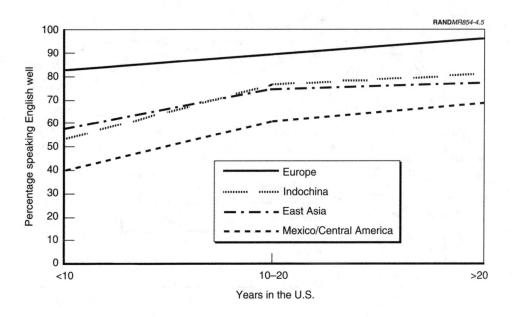

Figure 4.5—Immigrants from Different Countries Learn English at Different Rates

quent generations? Since we know that education is a good indicator of future earnings growth, we started there.

Figure 4.6 focuses on young adults of specific ethnic groups with at least some postsecondary education—i.e., adults age 25 to 34 who have completed at least 13 years of school—and compares them as to whether they are first-generation (immigrant) or subsequent-generation (native). Since the groups we chose have experienced large increases in immigration over the last two decades, many of those included as natives are likely to be children of immigrants. Clearly, the second generation makes significantly better progress in educating itself than the first generation does. The generational difference is especially pronounced for California's Hispanic-heritage population, but even so, the second-generation Mexicans and other second-generation Hispanics still greatly lag the other groups. To a considerable extent, this difference is a by-product of the educational levels of their immigrant parents, which are lower than those of the other groups' parents.

In sum, having a low level of education upon arrival in the United States means not only that the immigrants themselves will see reduced earnings, but that their offspring may need several generations to match the economic success of typical U.S. natives.

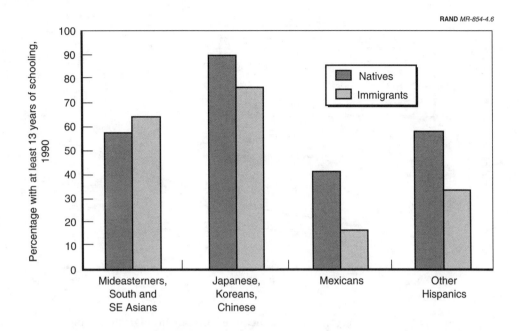

RAND *MR-854-4.6*

Figure 4.6—California's Subsequent Generations (Natives) Show Overall Gains in
Education, But Hispanics Still Lag Other Groups

But returns to education are not the same for all groups.

An individual's investment in additional education pays off in two ways. First,
more education results in a higher initial wage; second, this initial wage advantage is compounded by faster wage growth over the course of an individual's
career. This pattern holds for both immigrants and natives and for all ethnic
groups. Moreover, the more additional schooling the second generation com-
pletes relative to the first generation, the higher its relative wages will be. However, to shrink the earnings differentials for ethnic groups in the second and
subsequent generations, the returns to education must be equal for all groups.

Figure 4.7 demonstrates that the returns to education are not the same for all
groups. For natives, completing some college pays off about the same for Hispanics as it does for non-Hispanic whites. However, the story is different for a
college degree. The earnings of Hispanic college graduates at mid-career (age
45 to 54) are about 80 to 90 percent higher than those of Hispanics of the same
age who lack a high school diploma. The analogous gain for non-Hispanic
whites is at least 100 percent, and for Northeast Asians, it is even higher. Thus,
while a college education pays off for all groups, it pays off more for some than
for others.

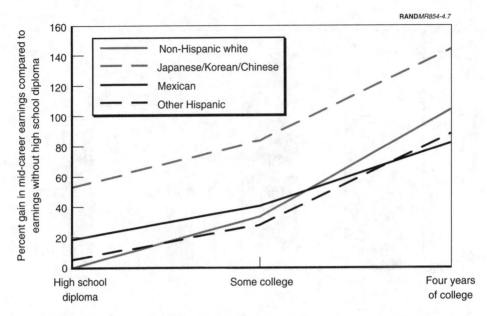

Figure 4.7—Economic Gains from Education Differ by Immigrant Heritage

Rates of naturalization vary among immigrant groups.

Naturalization is an important symbolic indicator of full participation in U.S. society. The longer immigrants stay in the United States, the more likely they are to become citizens. But, like other measures of integration, naturalization rates vary among immigrant groups (see Figure 4.8). Filipinos are the quickest to naturalize, whereas immigrants from regions close to the U.S. geographically (Mexico and Central America), socially (the United Kingdom), or both (Canada) are notably slower. Since 1990, however, naturalization rates have increased sharply—more than fourfold between 1993 and 1996—particularly for Mexican immigrants.

The Short Story

Immigrants from most places of origin appear to be attaining full participation in California's society and economy at least as fast as immigrants have histori- cally done. But the education and earnings of Hispanic immigrants—particu- larly those from Mexico—remain lower than those of other immigrant groups in both the first and the second generations.

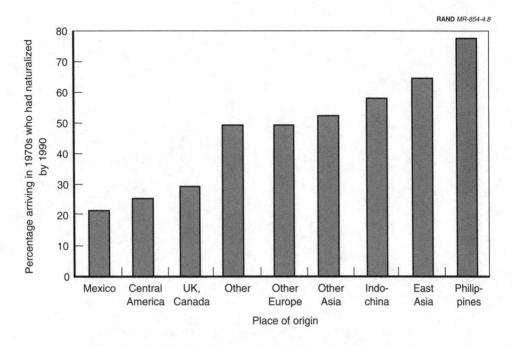

RAND *MR-854-4.8*

Figure 4.8—Immigrant Groups Naturalize at Different Rates

Chapter Five

Immigrants Increasingly Occupy the Bottom of the Labor Market

Context

California's labor market has been undergoing changes much like those in the national labor market. The new jobs created by the California economy are increasingly filled by workers who have attended college. While the number of jobs filled by workers lacking a high school diploma remained unchanged between 1970 and 1990, the California economy created 6.9 million new jobs, 85 percent of which went to workers with at least some college (see Figure 5.1). Clearly, the economic opportunities of workers are becoming increasingly differentiated by education. These trends (even more marked in the rest of the nation) suggest that the pool of low-skill jobs is shrinking, belying the widespread belief that California's past 20 to 30 years of "economic restructuring" expanded the number of jobs for less-educated workers.[1]

Question

What role do immigrants play in California's labor force?

Immigrants have contributed disproportionately to the growth of the state's labor force.

In contrast to the 1960s, when immigrants contributed only 10 percent of new entrants to California's labor force, the 1980s saw them contribute the majority—54 percent (see Figure 5.2). Outside California, immigrants represented a much smaller share of labor market growth—only 17 percent. Indeed, while

---

[1]As we indicate in the discussion that follows, these trends do not mean there are no longer jobs opening for workers with a high school education or less. The labor market is dynamic, with older, less-educated workers retiring, and adult workers upgrading their education and moving into new jobs. The jobs they leave are then filled by younger, less-educated, and often immigrant workers.

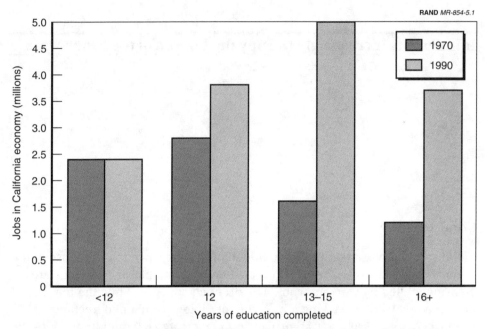

Figure 5.1—California's New Jobs Are Filled Primarily by Workers with at Least Some College Education

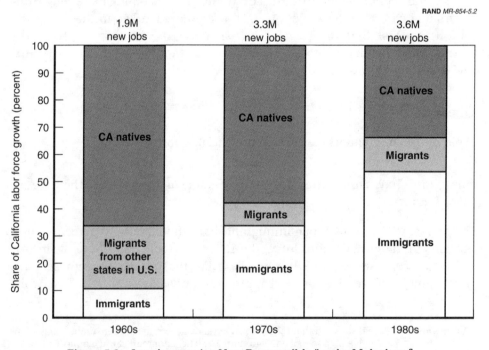

Figure 5.2—Immigrants Are Now Responsible for the Majority of California's Labor Force Growth

immigrants increased their share of California's labor force from 10 to 26 percent from 1970 to 1990, their share increased merely one percentage point—from 6 to 7 percent—in the rest of the country. Moreover, despite the fact that total employment in California failed to grow during the 1990–94 recession, immigrants continued to join the state's labor force at about the same rate as in the 1980s. Immigrants are now California's primary source of new labor.

Immigrants are replacing natives as the primary source of less-educated labor in California.

As older native workers retire and younger native adults enter the labor force with one or more years of college, immigrants are increasingly filling jobs that require less schooling. Figure 5.3 shows that immigrants filled 15 percent of the state's 2.4 million jobs held by workers without a high school diploma in 1970. By 1990, they filled 60 percent of those jobs, the total number of which has remained the same. They also filled about 67 percent of the 1 million new jobs taken by workers with only a high school diploma, but only about 20 percent of the 5.9 million new jobs taken by workers with one or more years of college.

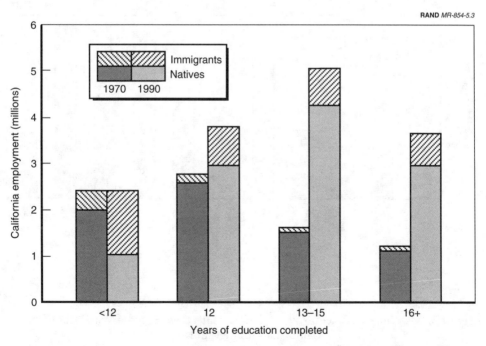

Figure 5.3—Immigrants Are Now the Primary Source of Labor for California Jobs
Requiring Less Than a High School Education

This outcome is largely a by-product of the increasing educational differential between California's immigrants and its natives. The gap in average educational levels between immigrants and natives increased from 1.8 years in 1970 to 2.6 years in 1990. Indeed, the failure of California's economy to create new low-skill jobs suggests that, within the next decade, few jobs will be available for new labor force entrants—native and foreign-born alike—who lack some postsecondary schooling.

Although all occupations now depend more on immigrant labor than they did in 1960, as Figure 5.4 shows, this dependence has been most striking at the lower end of the skill spectrum. For example, the immigrants' share of all executive, professional, and technical positions in California doubled between 1960 and 1990, but their share of operative, laborer, and other service jobs quintupled. Moreover, immigrants are less likely than natives to work in occupations requiring proficiency in English, such as sales and clerical positions. In the professional and technical fields, immigrants are more likely than natives to hold jobs in the scientific areas (e.g., engineering, health, computers) and less likely to hold jobs requiring certification in the United States (e.g., lawyers, teachers).

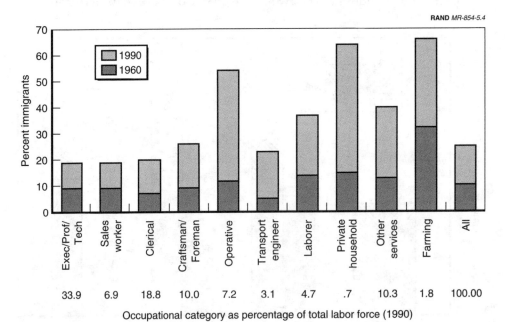

Figure 5.4—Occupations Requiring the Fewest Skills Have Become More Dependent on California's Immigrant Labor

The Short Story

California's economy has become progressively more reliant on immigrants overall, especially for filling low-skill jobs. However, since the number of such jobs in the state has not increased over the past 25 years (and has declined by 50 percent in the rest of the nation), the employment and earning prospects of Californians who lack the postsecondary schooling required for higher-skill jobs are narrowing.

Chapter Six

Immigration Has Contributed to California's Economic Growth

Context

As Figure 6.1 shows, from 1960 to 1990, California's total employment consistently grew more rapidly than the nation's total employment regardless of whether immigration levels were low (1960s) or high (1970s and 1980s). That situation changed during the recession of the early 1990s—the state lost some 450,000 jobs, suffering much more severely than the rest of the nation. Today, however, California job growth once again exceeds that of the rest of the nation.

Question

Has immigration contributed to California's disproportionate economic growth?

Immigrant labor has contributed to California's disproportionate growth.

Immigration contributed to the more rapid growth of California's economy between 1960 and 1990. We found a statistically significant, positive association between the rate of an industry's growth in California (relative to that industry's growth in the rest of the nation) and its dependence on immigrant labor. We made this comparison for 80 industries over three decades. Our analysis suggests that, on average, for every increase of five percentage points in the share of immigrants in a California industry's workforce (relative to the share for the industry's workforce in the rest of the country), total employment in that industry grew one percentage point faster in California than in the rest of the country.

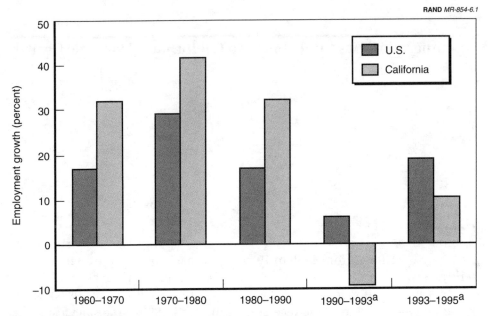

RAND *MR-854-6.1*

[a]Adjusted rates applicable over a ten-year period to make them comparable to the decennial rates from 1960 to 1990.

**Figure 6.1—Employment Has Consistently Grown Faster
in California Than in the Rest of the Nation**

Immigrants, though they earn less, are just as productive as native workers.

One main reason why immigration has had a positive effect on California's employment growth is the lower cost of immigrant, versus native, labor. As we demonstrated earlier, California natives have consistently outearned immigrants regardless of educational level. But immigrants' wages have also been falling relative to wages paid both to California natives and to immigrants and natives elsewhere in the United States—at least for workers having a high school diploma or less.

Figure 6.2 compares earnings within a predominantly low-skill industry (textiles and apparel) and a more high-skill industry (computer and accounting machine manufacturing).[1] In the case of the less-educated workers (high school diploma or less), California's immigrants have seen a decline in their wages relative to the wages of natives outside the state. For the more-educated workers,

---

[1]The pattern shown is generally consistent across all major manufacturing industries.

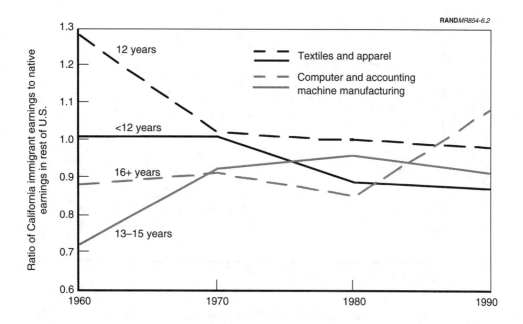

Figure 6.2—Trends in Most Immigrant Earnings Give California's Employers a Competitive Advantage

the results are mixed, but the earnings of California's immigrants have generally remained lower than those of natives elsewhere in the country. Other things being equal, these trends have been to the competitive advantage of California employers.

These lower earning patterns could simply mean that the productivity level of California's immigrants is lower than that of native workers. However, employers report preferring immigrants to other workers because they are "hard working," "motivated," and possess "a strong work ethic," and we found no evidence to support the proposition that immigrants are less productive. As Figure 6.3 shows, value added per manufacturing employee was 10 percent higher in California than in the rest of the nation in the 1960s and early 1970s, and although that advantage has eroded somewhat since then, it is still an advantage. Despite an increasing reliance on immigrants and, as the figure also shows, a somewhat lower level of capital investment per worker, California has maintained its productivity advantage.

In sum, California's employers have seen their labor costs decline relative to those of employers elsewhere in the United States and yet have not lost their productivity advantage.

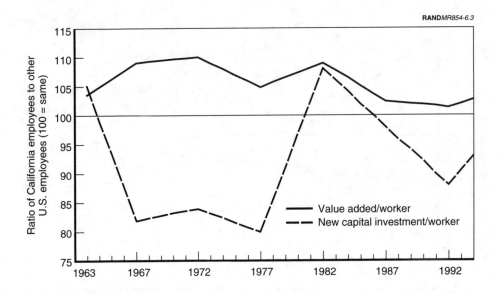

RAND*MR854-6.3*

Figure 6.3—Productivity of California's Manufacturing Workers
Remains Competitive

However, California's labor force has lost its educational advantage.

The disproportionate entry of immigrants with less than a high school education into California's labor force has caused it to lose the educational advantage
it once held over the rest of the country (see Figure 6.4). In 1960, the typical
California worker had almost one more year of education than the typical U.S.
worker did. In 1990, there was little difference. Moreover, immigration's effects
on the labor force's educational standing are not confined to the sharply dropping "Immigrant workers" curve in the figure: The relative decline in the educational level of California's natives reflects the lower educational attainment of
children born to immigrant parents in the state.

The Short Story

Immigrants have kept wages in California lower than those elsewhere in the
nation, causing employment in the state to grow at a faster rate than it would
have otherwise. However, the disproportionate entry of immigrants having less
than a high school education has led to the loss of the educational advantage
California's labor force traditionally held over the rest of the country. California's level of productivity has also dropped, but it is still higher than elsewhere
in the country. What remains to be seen is whether California will be able to

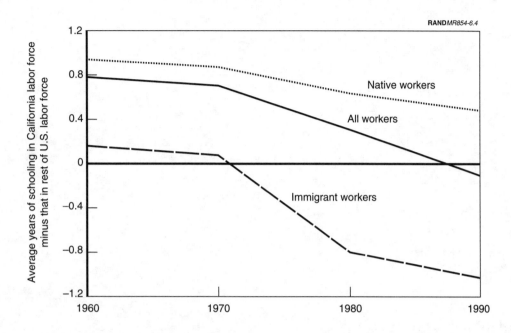

Figure 6.4—California's Labor Force Has Lost Its Educational Advantage

keep its productivity advantage over the long term if the educational level of its workers continues to decline relative to that of U.S. workers and capital investment per worker does not increase.

Chapter Seven

Immigration Has Adversely Affected Some Low-Skilled Workers—Both Native and Immigrant

Context

In its process of restructuring over the last few decades, the California economy has gone from being dominated by manufacturing to being dominated by service industries. This change has shifted the job skills needed for employment toward those requiring higher levels of education.

Figure 7.1 shows the two major effects these shifts have had on the labor force, the first of which concerns employment rates (left-hand graph). While the rates for male natives who attended college remained constant, the rates for those who did not attend college fell.[1] This drop was felt particularly among male African Americans and non-Mexican Hispanic Americans who did not complete high school. The employment rates for these groups fell from 57 percent in 1970 to 28 percent in 1990, compared to a drop from 68 to 47 percent for Mexican Americans with the same education.

The other major effect has been on weekly earnings (right-hand graph). While male natives who graduated from college increased their real earnings, all others earned less in real terms in 1990 than they had in 1970. These disparities are growing across the United States, but they are growing faster in California.

Question

Has immigration affected workers in California?

---

[1] From 1970 to 1990, the number of women working per 100 of working age grew across all levels of education, but grew more rapidly for the better educated.

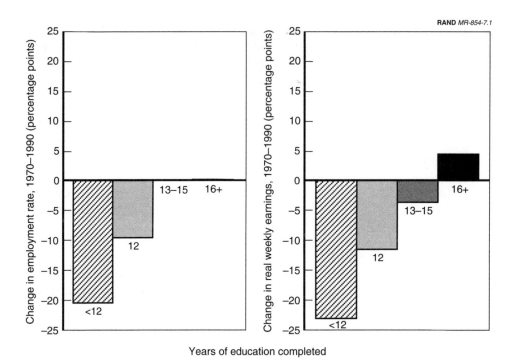

Figure 7.1—Employment Prospects and Earnings of Less-Educated Native Males
Dropped Relative to Those of the Better Educated from 1970 to 1990

Immigration has affected the job opportunities of a relatively small fraction of the California labor force.

Several factors could have contributed to the decline in employment rates, including competition from low-skilled labor abroad and an economy that increasingly requires more highly educated workers. We isolated immigration effects from these factors to estimate the effect that immigrants have had on employment in California.[2]

Perhaps 130,000 to 200,000 California natives were not in the labor force or were unemployed in 1990 because of immigration. This estimate represents roughly 1 to 1.5 percent of all natives of working age, and 3 to 5 percent of those either unemployed or not in the labor force. In addition, for every 20 to 30 additional immigrants working in California, there is one fewer native working.

---

[2]To isolate the effects of immigration from these other economic and labor market factors, we used two approaches. One involved comparing employment rate changes in California with those in the rest of the nation; the other involved a longitudinal analysis of the relation between employment rates and immigrants' share of the population across 124 metropolitan areas. Neither approach provided a definitive estimate, but the two produced generally consistent results.

Immigrants have contributed most to lowering the employment rate for high school dropouts, less to lowering it for high school graduates, and even less to lowering it for the college educated. In addition, their effect on employment rates has been felt more by some ethnic and gender groups than by others. Figure 7.2 shows some of our findings. The low boundary estimates indicate that immigration was responsible for 7 and 10 percent of the employment decline for, respectively, white American and Hispanic American males without a high school diploma. For similarly educated African American males, it was responsible for 16 percent of the decline.

It should be noted, however, that these figures assume no movement across state borders and thus may be underestimates.

Net migration from other states has declined in relative terms and has become more selective.

Net migration of U.S. workers to California fell about 30 percent between the late 1960s and late 1980s.[3] Relative net migration dropped by half between the

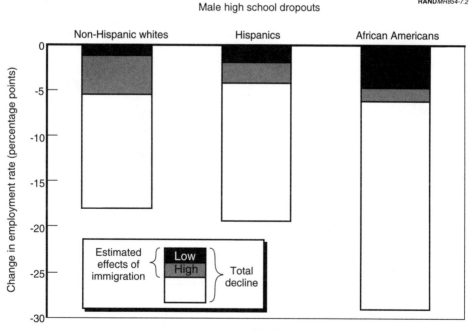

Figure 7.2—Immigration's Effect on the Employment Rate for Male High School Dropouts Varied for Different Groups from 1970 to 1990

---

[3]Net annual migration to California is the difference between the number of workers entering the state and the number of workers leaving the state.

1960s and 1970s—from 4.6 migrants per 1,000 California workers in the 1960s (when immigration was low), to 2.4 per 1,000 in the 1970s (when immigration had doubled). The net migration rate climbed back up, to 3.3 migrants per 1,000 workers, during the 1980s, when California's employment growth relative to the nation's was 50 percent greater than it had been in the 1970s. However, during the 1990–94 recession, when more people left California than entered it, the net migration rate was negative: The state lost six Californians annually for every 1,000 residents.

These migration flows were sharply differentiated by level of education (see Figure 7.3). In the late 1980s, for every 1,000 Californians not having a high school diploma, a net of 2.4 left the state annually. Meanwhile, for every 1,000 Californians with a college degree, six equally educated workers moved *into* the state from elsewhere in the country. Trends in interstate migration thus suggest that the California labor market continues to be attractive to the more-educated natives, but has become less attractive to the less educated.

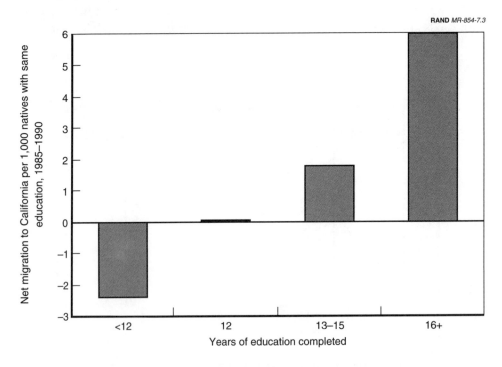

Figure 7.3—Net Migration of U.S. Workers to and from California Varied by Education from 1985 to 1990

Immigration reduced the earnings of less-educated workers only during the 1970s.

Immigration into California affected the earnings of less-educated natives in the 1970s, and it did so more for African and Hispanic Americans than for white Americans. For instance, we estimate that the earnings of African American males without a high school diploma would have been 10 to 16 percent—or $45 to $76 per week—higher had there been no immigration. Earnings of non-Hispanic white males would have been 4 to 8 percent higher—or $22 to $45 per week. This negative effect did not increase in the 1980s, and neither decade saw an adverse effect on the earnings of males who attended at least some college.[4]

Immigration also reduced the earnings of immigrants.

As Figure 7.4 shows, immigrants' earnings have declined more rapidly or increased less rapidly than those of natives. This effect stems partly from the fact

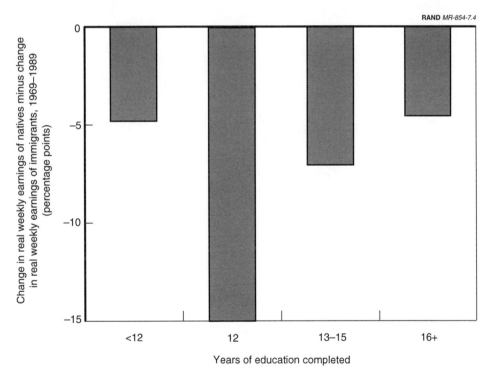

Figure 7.4—Earnings of Male Immigrants Declined More Than Those of Male Natives from 1970 to 1990

---

[4]The pattern for women was similar, though the adverse effect in the 1970s seemed to apply only to women who did not finish high school.

that nearly half of the total immigrants residing in California today arrived after 1980. As expected, the decline in immigrants' real wages relative to those of natives is most pronounced for workers having only a high school diploma.

The Short Story

Both the employment rates and real earnings of California natives with 12 years of education or fewer have generally declined over the past 20 years. This decline is the by-product of a restructuring economy, global competition, and stagnation in the growth of jobs for workers lacking a college education. Immigration, however, has also played a part in this decline by contributing to a slowdown in the net migration of Americans from other states. The earnings of immigrants have been even more affected than those of natives.

Chapter Eight

Immigrants Have Contributed to the Increased Demand for Public Services

Context

Since the late 1970s, California's voters have approved several initiatives aimed at curtailing the growth in per capita state and local revenues and limiting the legislature's ability to allocate revenues among services. As a result, California faced fiscal crises during the 1990–94 recession when the demand for services exceeded available revenues. Moreover, California continues to be confronted with difficult choices regarding how to fund higher education, corrections, and health and welfare programs. Cities and counties in the state are having to make similarly difficult decisions.

Question

Do immigrants put a disproportionate demand on public services?

Immigration is the main driver of increased enrollment in primary and secondary schools.

No public service in California has been more affected by immigration than education, a service primarily funded with state and local tax revenues. High levels of immigration since the 1960s have contributed to a reversal in what was a declining enrollment rate. As large numbers of children—both foreign-born and native—have entered school, K–12 enrollment has increased by one-third (see Figure 8.1).

The drop in enrollment shown for the 1970s would have been larger had it not been for the entrance of some 380,000 immigrant children. A comparable number of immigrant children entered during the 1980s, at the same time the number of native children under 12 increased by more than 1.1 million. And

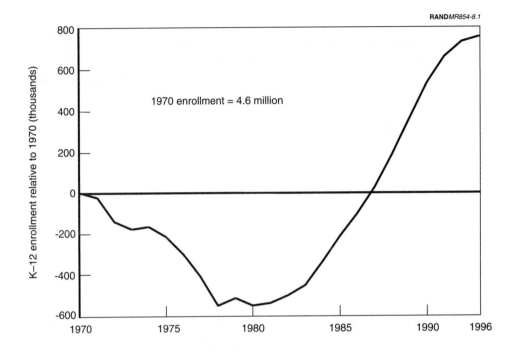

RAND*MR854-8.1*

Figure 8.1—Immigration Has Powered a Large Increase in
California School Enrollment

nearly half of that increase was due to children born in the United States to immigrant parents.

The full effect of immigration on postsecondary education has yet to be felt.

The number of high school graduates in California can be expected to increase by 30 to 40 percent over approximately the next ten years (see Figure 8.2). In addition, the race/ethnicity of high school graduates will change: Of the projected increase, two-thirds will be contributed by Asian (19 percent) and Hispanic (45 percent) youths.

Refugees are higher users of public services than are other immigrants.

Refugees, those immigrants admitted to the United States for humanitarian reasons, are more broadly eligible than other immigrants for public benefits immediately after arriving (see Figure 8.3). They are four times as likely as other immigrants to use Medicaid, six times as likely to obtain Aid to Families with Dependent Children (AFDC), and four times as likely to receive food stamps. In addition, refugees who are elderly are three times more likely than other elderly

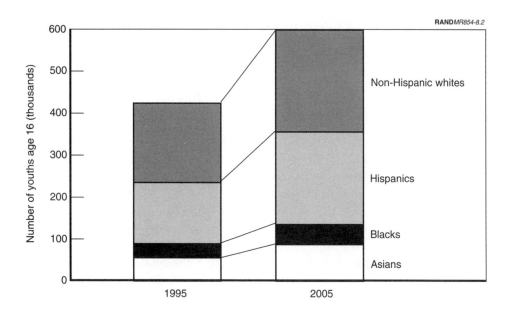

Figure 8.2—Immigration's Effect on California Postsecondary Education Will Increase over the Next Decade

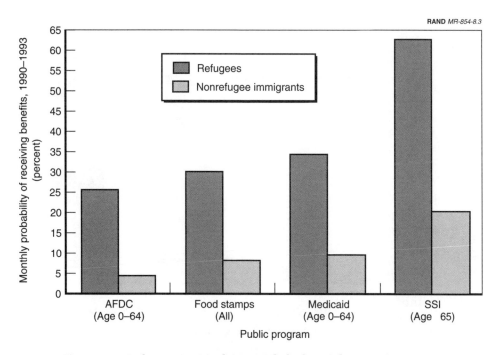

Figure 8.3—Refugees Are Much More Likely than Other Immigrants to Receive Public Benefits

immigrants to receive Supplemental Security Insurance (SSI) benefits. This higher use of benefits by refugees is especially important in California, home to a disproportionate share—44 percent—of the refugees admitted to the United States.

Elderly immigrants are more likely than elderly natives to use "safety net" programs.

Figure 8.4 compares public-program use for elderly natives with that for elderly immigrants, a rapidly growing segment of the immigrant population. As can be seen, of these two groups, immigrants are more likely to use the safety net programs: They are three times as likely to rely on SSI benefits, and more than twice as likely to participate in the Medicaid program. At the same time, they are less likely to benefit from the two federal social insurance programs for the elderly—Social Security and Medicare—because they have not accumulated enough years in the labor market (many come to reunite with grown children living in the United States) to qualify for these federal programs, or because they are receiving minimal benefits that need to be augmented with SSI benefits. Since Social Security and Medicare are fully funded by the federal govern-

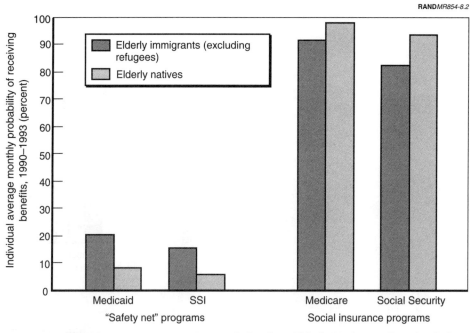

Figure 8.4—Elderly Immigrants Are More Likely Than Elderly Natives to Receive Safety Net Benefits

ment (through employee and employer payroll tax deductions), and SSI and Medicaid are partially funded with state general resources, this pattern of service use by elderly immigrants disproportionately affects the states.

Overall, immigrants who are neither refugees nor elderly are no more likely than natives to use public services.

We found no significant differences between natives and nonrefugee/ nonelderly immigrants in terms of their participation in a wide range of cash assistance, nutrition, health, and housing programs in the 1991–93 period (see Figure 8.5). In fact, for families earning less than $16,000 annually, immigrants were 30 percent less likely than natives to use AFDC, 20 percent less likely to receive food stamps, and 30 percent less likely to use the Medicaid program. The one exception is the school lunch and breakfast programs: Children of immigrant parents are nearly twice as likely to participate as are children of native parents. This pattern of use reflects the overall lower incomes, larger family sizes, and, in particular, larger number of children in immigrant versus native families.

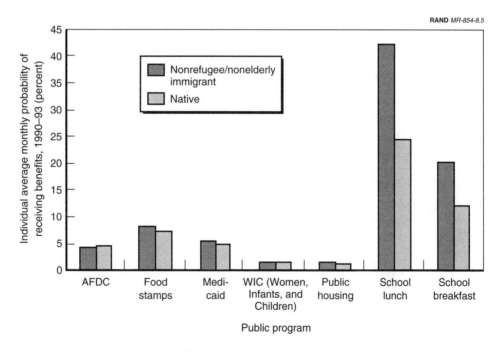

Figure 8.5—Nonrefugee/Nonelderly Immigrants Are No More Likely Than Natives to Receive Benefits from Public Programs

California disproportionately bears the costs of providing public services to immigrants.

Because California has more immigrants per capita than the rest of the country, California residents pay more immigration costs than do residents of other states. In addition, the ratio of refugees to nonrefugee immigrants is higher in California than in other states, and California's immigrants have larger families and lower incomes. These additional factors make the average cost per immigrant higher in California, which raises the cost per California resident.

California also has proportionately more elderly immigrants than other states do, as well as a higher proportion of young immigrants and young children of immigrants, all of whom rely heavily on services primarily funded by state and local governments. Because these factors all operate in the same direction, they reinforce each other, leading to higher immigrant use of public service programs and lower tax revenues from immigrants in California than in the rest of the nation.[1]

The Short Story

Education is where immigration has had the most pronounced effect on public services in California. And the full effects of immigration have yet to be felt by the state's high schools and colleges. Although most immigrants are no more likely than natives to use social safety net programs, the high proportion of refugees and of elderly and low-educated immigrants in California compared to the rest of the nation has contributed to the disproportionate fiscal cost of immigration for California and its localities.

---

[1]A recent study by the National Research Council (*The New Americans: Economic, Demographic, and Fiscal Effects of Immigration*, Washington, D.C.: National Academy Press, 1997) estimated that the net state/local fiscal deficit for providing services to immigrants in 1996 was $1,178 per native household in California compared to $232 per native household in New Jersey.

Chapter Nine

Immigration Policies Should Be More Flexible and Encourage the Integration of Immigrants

Overall, California continues to benefit from immigration. But the growing divergence between the state's economy and the qualifications of immigrant workers is creating costs to the state, its residents, and the immigrants themselves. The nation's immigration policies, which are based on fixed regulations, quotas, and preferences that are applied in all circumstances, is no longer responsive to today's workplace. We believe the goal of federal immigration policy should be to regulate the volume and characteristics of the immigrant population so as to maximize the benefits to everyone and minimize adverse effects.

We also believe that California should develop more-effective policies for integrating the immigrants who are already here, a group that constitutes about a quarter of the state's population. The state government should take steps to reduce immigration's long-term costs and increase its long-term benefits.

This chapter presents more detailed recommendations for both federal and state policy.

Federal Policy

Allow easier, more frequent changes to immigration regulations.

The nature of immigration flows and the receiving environment can change dramatically in a short span of time. Currently, legal immigration is regulated with inflexible laws that Congress typically amends every 10 to 15 years. Laws should be authorized for shorter periods, or the executive branch should be allowed more flexibility to responsively manage immigration policy within broad policy parameters as to how many and which immigrants should be admitted annually.

Maintain overall immigration levels within a moderate range.

Current immigration policy establishes a fixed annual level of legal admissions. This fixed limit typically operates as a floor rather than a ceiling, because certain entrants are exempt from the overall limit and because refugee admissions are adjusted annually to accommodate international conditions. As a result, the number of annual admissions has been increasing. The costs of providing public services to immigrants and the economic effects of immigrants on current residents (both natives and earlier immigrants) vary depending on U.S. economic conditions. One result of this dependence is that a backlash against all immigration can occur when the American public perceives that immigration levels are too high.

A more balanced approach would be to adjust the total number of entrants so that it falls within a moderate annual range, depending on current economic conditions, and incorporate within that range annual refugee admissions. Defining what constitutes a "moderate" range is, of course, open to debate, but something between the 800,000 per year that occurred during the early 1990s and the 400,000 per year of the 1970s would provide a reasonable starting place. Moreover, incorporating refugee admissions within the annual ceiling would permit policymakers to adjust the balance between legal and refugee admissions to accommodate changing domestic and international conditions without exceeding the overall total.

Increase the educational levels of new immigrants.

In a society whose demand for more-educated workers is growing, the effect of admitting immigrants who are significantly less educated than natives is to put those immigrants at a disadvantage that can take generations to overcome. The federal government should expand the criteria used to determine admission eligibility to include (in addition to family reunification) educational level and work skills.

Support programs designed to expedite English proficiency.

Although the vast majority of immigrants who remain in the United States eventually learn English, some groups seriously lag others in terms of how long the process takes. The importance of a rapid acquisition of English for economic success and integration is widely recognized, and immigrants themselves believe it is important to attain English proficiency. Maintaining the English-language requirements for naturalization and providing funding for English-language education are two ways the federal government can ease the integration of immigrants into California's society and economy. In turn, California should be ready to complement and, if necessary, supplement federal efforts.

Recognize that illegal immigration is an issue of values, not effects.

Currently, the public seems to be in favor of much more rigorous laws to limit illegal immigration. The traditional problem with regard to illegal immigration, however, has been one of insufficient enforcement rather than inadequate regulation. This problem stems primarily from a lack of consensus among policymakers, not from the performance of the Immigration and Naturalization Service. Underlying this situation has been a tendency to focus on the issue of illegal immigration in terms of its effects: So long as its effects are viewed as positive, illegal immigration is not regarded as a major problem. Indeed, some people have advocated that illegal immigration should be governed by market forces rather than regulations.

But a full accounting of the costs and benefits of illegal immigration is probably impossible. Moreover, the central concern with regard to illegal immigration is not simply one of effects. Failure to rigorously enforce the nation's laws for illegal immigration has three negative effects on American values. First of all, it encourages a disregard for immigration law and perhaps for the rule of law more generally. Second, it violates basic equity principles with regard to potential immigrants who play by the rules and wait for their turn. And third, it encourages a backlash against all immigration and immigrants.

Expand bilateral cooperation with Mexico on immigration issues.

Immigration from Mexico is clearly a special case. Mexico provides almost 50 percent of all California's immigrants and is the primary source of illegal immigration into the United States. In addition, Mexican immigrants are typically among the least educated and have the lowest incomes of all immigrant groups. However, large numbers of California's Mexican Americans have close family ties with Mexican nationals. Additionally, both California and the United States share with Mexico a wide range of economic, environmental, social, and political interests, and Mexico has a high economic and social stake in seeing its emigration flows continue.

In sum, the issue of Mexican immigration cannot be divorced from the broader context of U.S.–Mexico relations, regardless of how much the U.S. and Mexican governments might like it to be. Both countries must realize the special role Mexican immigration to the United States plays in their national lives. Moreover, both need to recognize their direct interest in ensuring that the immigrant flows continue, but that they do so at a controlled rate. What is needed is for the United States to treat Mexico differently than it treats other countries. In particular, efforts should be made to develop greater bilateral cooperation on immigration matters. This might entail expanding the number of legal residence permits available for Mexican immigrants in exchange for Mexican government collaboration on U.S.-Mexico border enforcement.

Review the allocation of costs between federal and state governments.

Although immigration is preeminently a federal responsibility, there is little question that the states often feel the impact of immigration policies most directly. The federal government must be willing to consider ways to alleviate the costs its immigration policies impose on state and local governments.

Specifically, the federal government should consider making broad compensation to California for its immigration costs. The state has no control over immigration policy, and yet immigration's net costs over the short term are more negative at the state level than at the federal level. We recognize that justly allocating costs between the federal and state levels touches on beliefs about federal and state roles that are beyond the bounds of objective analysis. However, our recommendation is based on the idea that by accepting more of the cost of its own actions, the federal government can help ensure that both it and California will make choices serving the national interest.

State Policy

Encourage naturalization.

Just as is true for other states, California can more easily balance the interests of all of its residents if those who are not yet citizens become citizens. But naturalization is a very slow process, slower for some immigrant groups than for others. The federal government recently began moving from a laissez-faire policy on naturalization toward more-active facilitation. We endorse this shift in approach and recommend that it be continued.

Ensure equality of educational opportunity through college.

Our results show that many immigrants and their offspring, especially Hispanics, are losing ground in educational attainment to other immigrant groups and to natives. If Californians want to sustain a single, integrated society, they will have to alter the state's trend toward disinvesting in education, particularly higher education. Special efforts should be undertaken to encourage high school graduation and college attendance within the Hispanic community and to discover ways to enhance the educational achievement of Hispanics.

Establish a state office of immigrant affairs.

As Proposition 187 and its aftermath have demonstrated, immigration has the potential to exacerbate existing divisions within California, the nation's most populous and most socially diverse state. Responsible leaders within the state should take action to see that this does not happen, since it could well have serious negative consequences for the state's economic, social, and political fabric.

Though elected officials and state bureaucrats respond to the interests of particular racial and ethnic groups, no one state agency or representative appears to consider the effects of government policies on immigrants per se. Nor is any one person or group responsible for California natives' concerns about how immigrants are affecting them. Moreover, despite the diverse effects that immigrants have on the state's public and private sectors, there is no agency within the state that monitors and coordinates immigration issues. The state should consider establishing an independent office of immigrant affairs that would have three principal functions: monitor the needs and position of immigrants, track the impact of immigrants on society, and coordinate state policies having to do with immigrants.

Increase public understanding of immigration issues.

A continued widening of the educational and economic gaps now existing between California's immigrants and natives will have implications for other divisions within the state. An increasing generation gap pits programs for the education and welfare of children against programs for the elderly, such as Medicare and Social Security. This division between young and old is exacerbated by a young population of immigrants and their children and an aging native population. California's current debate about affirmative action is partly fueled by perceived competition between newcomers and earlier generations. And Southern and Northern California's historical competition over resources and political power may be compounded by the fact that Southern California has a disproportionate number of immigrants. Finally, the growing economic disparity between those who have a higher education and those who do not has added a new economic dimension to this mix.

To summarize, it is particularly important that Californians have a clear understanding of immigration issues and their implications. We hope this report contributes to that understanding.